CONTINENTS

Asia

Michael and Jane Pelusey

CHELSEA HOUSE
PUBLISHERS

A Haights Cross Communications ◆ Company

www.chelseahouse.com

This edition first published in 2005 in the United States of America by Chelsea House Publishers, a subsidiary of Haights Cross Communications.

Chelsea House Publishers
2080 Cabot Blvd West, Suite 201
Langhorne, PA 19047-1813

The Chelsea House world wide web address is www.chelseahouse.com

First published in 2004 by
MACMILLAN EDUCATION AUSTRALIA PTY LTD
627 Chapel Street, South Yarra 3141

Visit our website at www.macmillan.com.au

Associated companies and representatives throughout the world.

Library of Congress Cataloging-in-Publication Data
Pelusey, Michael.
    Asia / by Michael and Jane Pelusey.
    p. cm. – (Continents)
    Includes index.
    ISBN 0-7910-8280-6
    1. Asia – Juvenile literature. I. Pelusey, Jane. II. Title.
    DS5.P38 2004
    915'.02–dc22

                                                    2004015815

Edited by Angelique Campbell-Muir
Text design by Karen Young
Cover design by Karen Young
Illustrations by Nina Sanadze
Maps by Laurie Whiddon, Map Illustrations

Printed in China

Acknowledgments
The author and the publisher are grateful to the following for permission to
reproduce copyright material:

Cover photographs: Japanese Temple, courtesy of PhotoEssentials. Tiger, courtesy of ANT Photo
Library.

All photographs © Pelusey Photography except for Artville, pp. 22, 24, 26 (left);
Digital Vision, p. 26 (right); Helen Fielding, p. 10 (top); Image Box, p. 20; June Horner,
p. 23 (top); John and Marina Suthers, p. 23 (bottom).

While every care has been taken to trace and acknowledge copyright, the publisher tenders
their apologies for any accidental infringement where copyright has proved untraceable.
Where the attempt has been unsuccessful, the publisher welcomes information that would
redress the situation.

Please note
At the time of printing, the Internet addresses appearing in this book were correct.
Owing to the dynamic nature of the Internet, however, we cannot guarantee that all
these addresses will remain correct.

Contents

Glossary words

When a word is printed in **bold**, you can look up its meaning in the Glossary on page 31.

Asia is a continent

Asia is the largest continent in the world. Look at a world map or globe and you can see that the world is made up of water and land. The big areas of land are called continents. There are seven continents:

- Africa
- Antarctica
- Asia
- Australia
- Europe
- North America
- South America.

Borders

The borders of continents follow natural physical features such as coastlines and mountain ranges. Asia's sea borders are the:

- Indian Ocean
- Pacific Ocean
- Arctic Ocean.

Asia is attached to Europe. Sometimes Asia and Europe together are called Eurasia. The Asian-European border divides Russia and Turkey in two, so both countries are in Asia and Europe. The Asian-European border runs along the:

- Ural Mountains
- Ural River
- Caspian Sea.

World map showing the seven modern-day continents

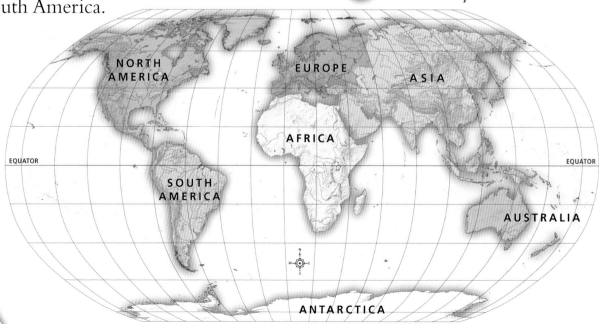

The world is a jigsaw

The Earth's crust is made up of huge plates, called **tectonic plates**, which fit together like a jigsaw puzzle. These plates are constantly moving, up and down and sideways, up to 4 inches (10 centimeters) a year. Over long periods of time, the plates change in size and shape as their edges push against each other.

Around 250 million years ago, there was one massive supercontinent called Pangaea. Around 200 million years ago, it began splitting and formed two continents. Laurasia was the northern continent and Gondwana was the southern continent. By about 65 million years ago, Laurasia and Gondwana had separated into smaller landmasses that look much like the continents we know today. Laurasia split to form Europe, Asia, and North America. Gondwana split to form South America, Africa, Australia, and Antarctica.

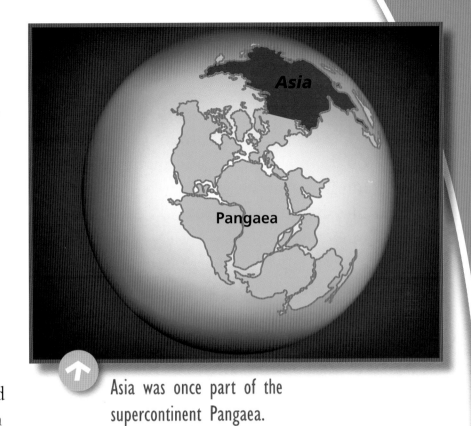

Asia was once part of the supercontinent Pangaea.

The Asian continent formed when Laurasia split into smaller landmasses.

Early Asia

When the continents were one, animals moved across the land, as there was no water to stop them. When the continents split apart, the animals were left on separate landmasses and they began to change and develop into the animals we know today. During this time, dinosaurs roamed the Earth, including Asia. As the dinosaurs became **extinct**, other animals took over. An elephant-like animal called a woolly mammoth lived in the cold northern parts of Asia. It had long hair to keep warm and long ivory tusks.

Early humans

Scientists believe modern humans, or *Homo sapiens*, came from Africa and then made their way to Asia around 50,000 years ago.

Woolly mammoths died out 4,000 years ago.

↑ Angkor in Cambodia was built from 800–1,000 years ago.

First civilizations

Early humans in Africa discovered how to grow crops such as wheat and barley. Groups of humans moved together to help each other grow crops and for protection. Eventually, small settlements grew into towns and cities, which became the start of early civilizations.

Early cities developed in West Asia around 8,000 years ago. This area was called Mesopotamia. These people were part of the great Persian Empire. Around 3,500 years ago, Chinese civilizations began to grow. They built cities that stretched along the huge rivers in the area.

Early Asian civilizations

⊕ Mesopotamia (8,000 years ago) farmed and built simple cities.

⊕ Chinese Shang and Chou dynasties (3,500 to 2,200 years ago) farmed and **traded**.

⊕ Indus Valley in India (3,500 years ago) farmed and traded.

⊕ Persians (2,500 years ago) built iron weapons.

⊕ Chin Dynasty (2,200 years ago) started building the Great Wall of China.

⊕ Khmer of Angkor (1,000 years ago) built the temple-city of Angkor in Cambodia.

The Great Wall of China was completed during the Ming Dynasty (1368–1644).

Asia today

A village farm in the highlands of Asia

Asia is the world's biggest continent. It covers an area of 16.8 million square miles (43.6 million square kilometers). Asia is made up of 49 countries, including Russia and Turkey, which are in both Asia and Europe. The largest country is Russia, which has an area of 6.5 million square miles (17 million square kilometres). Almost 5 million square miles (13 million square kilometers) of Russia is in Asia. The smallest countries in Asia are the Maldives, at 116 square miles (300 square kilometers), and Bahrain, at 239 square miles (620 square kilometers). Both the Maldives and Bahrain are groups of islands.

The physical features of the Asian contintent

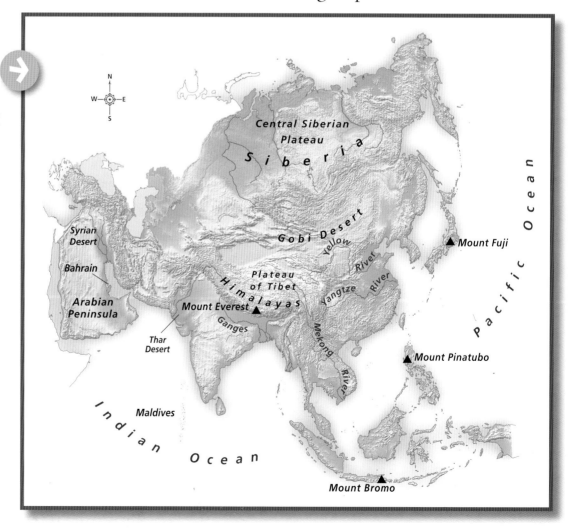

8

There are many volcanoes in Indonesia. This one is in Bali.

Physical features

Asia is in the **Northern Hemisphere**. The northern part of Asia lies inside the **Arctic Circle**. South of the Arctic Circle are flat areas of low land called plains. Some of these plains are dry deserts. There are also plains high above the level of the sea, called plateaus. Between the plains and deserts are mountain ranges. Huge rivers flow from mountain ranges through plains to the ocean. There are many islands in Southeast Asia. They are mainly volcanic.

Asian people

Asia has more people than any other continent. The 3.8 billion people who live in Asia make up more than half of the world's total population. Asian people can be divided into many **ethnic groups** with different languages, **traditions**, and religions.

The markets in Myanmar are a busy meeting place for locals.

9

The land

Asia is such a big continent that it has many different landforms.

Mountains

Many of the highest mountains in the world are in the Himalayan Mountains. There are 200 peaks above 19,684 feet (6,000 meters) in the Himalayas. The nearby Tibetan Platcau has an average height of 13,123 feet (4,000 meters), which makes it the highest plateau in the world.

Many adventurers climb the Himalayan Mountains.

Highest mountain

Mount Everest is the highest mountain in the world. It is 29,030 feet (8,848 meters) high. It is situated on the border between Nepal and China, in the Himalayas.

Volcanoes

Volcanoes, such as Indonesia's Mount Bromo and the Philippines' Mount Pinatubo, often erupt smoke and molten rock called lava. Erupting volcanoes and earthquakes have killed thousands of people in Asia. Some volcanoes, such as Mount Fuji in Japan, are dormant or extinct.

Mount Fuji in Japan is covered in snow during the winter.

Deserts

The Gobi Desert in China is on a high plateau. High land is colder than low land, so the Gobi is called a cold desert. Hot deserts are found in western Asia, such as on the Arabian Peninsula. India also has an area of hot dry land called the Thar Desert.

Camels are used for transportation in the Thar Desert.

Islands

Indonesia is the biggest group of islands in the world. Other Asian countries that are made up of groups of islands include the Philippines, Japan, and Sri Lanka.

The Yangtze River is a major transportation route. This ship is carrying coal.

Rivers

Asia has many big rivers, such as the Mekong, Ganges, Yangtze, Yellow, and Irrawaddy. Many people live on the banks of these rivers and use the water for farming and transporting goods on boats.

Asia's longest river

The longest river in Asia is the Yangtze in China. It is 3,965 miles (6,380 kilometers) long. It is the third longest river in the world after the Nile and Amazon.

The climate

Asia is a big continent with a huge range of climates. Temperatures get warmer the closer the countries are to the **equator**.

Arctic

Winters in northern Asia are very cold. Temperatures in Russia can drop below −22 degrees Fahrenheit (−30 degrees Celsius). Summers in the north are brief so people there only have a short time to grow crops. This is known as an **arctic** climate.

Alpine

The Himalayan Mountains are high enough to have snow and ice on their peaks all year round. This is known as an **alpine** climate. The weather in these mountains can change from sunny and warm to stormy and freezing within minutes. Many mountain climbers have died on Mount Everest because they were caught in sudden bad weather.

Temperate

Most of southern Japan, South Korea, and parts of eastern China have a **temperate** climate. They get warm wet summers and cool to cold winters.

This lake in South Korea has frozen over.

Climate zones in Asia

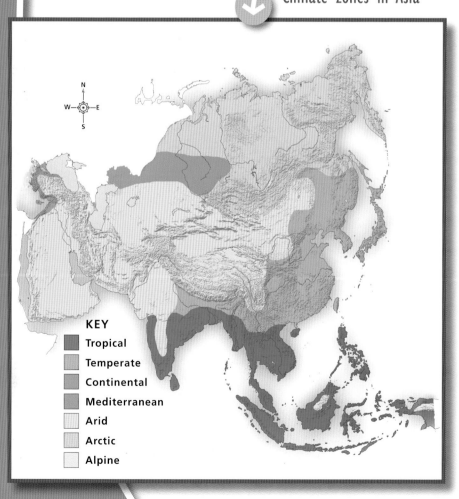

KEY
- Tropical
- Temperate
- Continental
- Mediterranean
- Arid
- Arctic
- Alpine

↑ A thunderstorm builds up over the Mekong River in Luang Prabang, Laos.

Continental

The sea has an even temperature that helps to keep coastal places from getting too hot or too cold. Places far from the coast have a **continental** climate. These parts of Asia that are farther from the sea get less rain, very cold winters, and hot summers.

Arid

It hardly ever rains in an **arid** or desert climate. Some deserts, such as the Gobi, are cold with winter temperatures dropping to below −22 degrees Fahrenheit (−30 degrees Celsius). The Thar Desert in India is a hot desert. It can reach temperatures of more than 122 degrees Fahrenheit (50 degrees Celsius) in summer.

Tropical and monsoon

Indonesia is on the equator, so it is hot and **humid** all year round with heavy rain. Farther away from the equator it is still **tropical**, but there are separate dry and wet seasons. This **monsoon** climate is found in India and Southeast Asia.

The wettest month ever recorded
Once, 366 inches (9,300 millimeters) of rain fell in Cherrapunji, India, in just one month.

13

Plants and animals

Asia has many thousands of different plants and animals. The greatest numbers of plants and animals are found in the hot, wet tropical rain forests of Southeast Asia. The Arctic has the fewest numbers of animals because it is so cold.

Arctic

Arctic animals and plants have learned to live in the very cold conditions. Small flowering plants come out during the short spring and summer seasons, which provide food for herds of reindeer in Siberia. Most of the year these plants are covered in snow.

Forests

Farther south, where the climate is milder, forest trees grow taller. Forests in China often have areas of bamboo. Bamboo is a type of tall grass with a long straight stem. The giant panda, a black and white bear-like animal, eats only bamboo.

Pandas live only in China. They are becoming very rare as bamboo and forest areas are cleared for farming.

The tiger's stripes make it hard to see in tall grass.

Orangutans are becoming rare in the wild because of forest clearing and hunting.

Tropical rain forest

Many tall trees grow close together in the tropical rain forests of Southeast Asia. These trees block out the sun and stop it from reaching the forest floor. Only plants that like shade, such as palms and ferns, grow there. Many animals live in the forest canopy, high up in the branches of trees. The orangutan is a large ape that eats fruit and sleeps in tall trees.

The world's largest cat, the tiger, lives in the rain forests of Thailand and the plains of India. Tigers hunt deer and small animals for food. Elephants also live in the rain forests. In countries such as Thailand and Myanmar, tame elephants are sometimes used to drag heavy logs.

The rafflesia flower attracts flies to pollinate it.

Giant flower

One of the world's biggest flowers is found in the rain forests of Malaysia and Indonesia. The rafflesia flower is nearly 3 feet (1 meter) wide.

The people

Over half of all the world's people live in Asia. Since much of Asia is made up of mountains and deserts, most people live on the plains. These areas are very crowded in places.

Ethnic groups

Asians belong to many different ethnic groups. Some ethnic groups are big, such as the Han Chinese with over one billion people. Other ethnic groups, such as the Hmong and Akha who live in Thailand's mountain villages, are much smaller. These smaller ethnic groups are called minorities.

People facts	
Population	3.8 billion people
Most populated country	China with 1.3 billion people
Least populated country	Maldives with 360,000 people
Most crowded country	Singapore with 15,285 people per square mile (5,902 people per square kilometer)

Biggest populations
China has the most people of any country in the world. By 2030, India may pass China and become the country with the most people. Both countries have more than one billion people each.

These Chinese children belong to the Han group.

16

Languages

The people of Asia speak many different languages. They also have their own ways of writing. People from China and Korea write using groups of characters that are pictures. Arabic, Thai, and Khmer languages also use different alphabets.

An Islamic **mosque** in Brunei

Religion

Many religions first began in Asia. Various countries have different forms of each religion. Some of the religions that began in Asia are:

- Islam, in Saudi Arabia
- Hinduism, in India
- Buddhism, in India
- Christianity
- Judaism, in Israel
- Sikhism, in India
- Confucianism and Taoism, in China.

People worshiping in a Buddhist temple in Laos

The countries

There are 49 countries in Asia, many of which are islands. Asia can be divided into the following regions:

- 🌐 North Asia
- 🌐 West Asia
- 🌐 South Asia
- 🌐 Southeast Asian Islands.

Colonies

From the 1700s, people from European countries such as England, France, the Netherlands, Portugal, and Spain were exploring the world. They wcre looking for new lands and valuable goods such as gold and spices. Explorers often stayed and **colonized** countries, for example, India, Indonesia, and Malaysia. Some Asian countries wanted more land so they invaded nearby countries. Japan invaded China and Korea, and later occupied most of Southeast Asia during World War II (1939–1945). Russia, too, once controlled many of its neighbors. Colonial power influenced language, architecture, and traditions. Most Asian countries became **independent** after World War II.

French bread for sale in Vietnam

RUSSIA
GEORGIA
TURKEY
CYPRUS
ARMENIA
AZERBAIJAN
LEBANON
ISRAEL
SYRIA
KAZAKHSTAN
MONGOLIA
JORDAN
IRAQ
TURKMENISTAN
UZBEKISTAN
NORTH KOREA
JAPAN
IRAN
KYRGYZSTAN
SAUDI ARABIA
KUWAIT
AFGHANISTAN
TAJIKISTAN
SOUTH KOREA
BAHRAIN
QATAR
PAKISTAN
NEPAL
CHINA
UNITED ARAB EMIRATES
OMAN
BHUTAN
YEMEN
TAIWAN
INDIA
MYANMAR
BANGLADESH
LAOS
PHILIPPINES
THAILAND
VIETNAM
CAMBODIA
SRI LANKA
BRUNEI
MALDIVES
MALAYSIA
SINGAPORE
INDONESIA
EAST TIMOR

KEY
- North Asia
- South Asia
- West Asia
- Southeast Asian Islands

Asian regions and countries

18

Asian wars

Asia has had many wars. Around 2,500 years ago, Mongols and Chinese fought over land, until the Chinese eventually built the Great Wall of China to stop the Mongol invasions. Many Asian people died during World War II, which ended in 1945 when American forces dropped two atomic bombs on the cities of Hiroshima and Nagasaki in Japan. Other wars involving Asia include the Korean War (1950–1953) and the Vietnam War (1961–1975). Neighboring countries India and Pakistan have been fighting over who owns the land of Kashmir. Iran, Iraq, Afghanistan, and Israel have fought many wars over the last 50 years.

The newest country

East Timor is the world's newest country. It was part of Indonesia until 2002 when, after years of fighting for freedom, the East Timorese **voted** for independence.

A fighter plane used during the Korean War

North Asia

There are 12 countries in North Asia. Use the key below to find out about and compare each country's languages, religions, ethnic groups, agriculture, and natural resources.

Country	Languages	Religions	Ethnic groups	Agriculture	Natural resources
China					
Japan					
Kazakhstan					
Kyrgyzstan					
Mongolia					
North Korea					
Russia					
South Korea					
Taiwan					
Tajikistan					
Turkmenistan					
Uzbekistan					

Key

Languages	Religions	Ethnic groups	Agriculture	Natural resources
Cantonese Chinese	Buddhism	Han Chinese	Cereal grains	Bauxite or alumina
English	Christianity	Japanese	Cotton	Coal
Japanese	Islam	Kazakh	Dairy	Copper
Kazakh	Shinto	Korean	Fruit and vegetables	Gold
Korean	Taoism	Kyrgyz	Peanuts	**Hydropower**
Kyrgyz		Minority groups	Sheep, cattle, and goats	Iron ore
Mandarin Chinese		Mongolian	Sugar beet	Lead
Mongol		Russian	Tea	Nickel
Russian		Tajik	Wine and grapes	Oil and gas
Tajik		Turkmen		Phosphates
Traditional languages		Uzbek		Salt
Turkmen				Silver
Uzbek				Timber
				Tin
				Uranium
				Zinc

China in focus

Official name: People's Republic of China

Area: 3,600,927 square miles
(9,326,410 square kilometers)

Population: 1.3 billion

Capital: Beijing

Major cities: Shanghai, Chengdu, Guangzhou,
Tianjin, Chongqing, Wuhan, Hong Kong

Famous landmarks: Great Wall of China,
Forbidden Palace, Terracotta Warriors,
Yangtze River, Tiananmen Square in Beijing

Famous people: Mao Zedong, Deng Xiaoping
(political leaders)

Traditions: fireworks, tai chi (martial art),
mah-jongg (game), calligraphy

Traditional food: steamed buns stuffed with meat and vegetables,
Peking duck, rice, noodles

There are many rice
fields in southern China.

China is the second biggest country in Asia. China has more people than any other
country in the world. The mighty Yangtze and Yellow rivers wind through the
countryside providing water for crops. Mount Everest, the highest mountain in the
world, is on the border of China and Nepal.

Japan in focus

Official name: Japan

Area: 145,374 square miles
(376,520 square kilometers)

Population: 127 million

Capital: Tokyo

Major cities: Yokohama, Kyoto, Osaka, Nagoya,
Kobe, Fukuoka

Famous landmarks: Mount Fuji

Famous people: Emperor Hirohito

Traditions: tea ceremony, sumo wrestling, origami (paper folding),
bonsai (miniature tree growing), judo (martial art)

Traditional food: sushi, sashimi (raw fish), tempura (battered and
deep-fried vegetables and seafood)

The fast bullet train
travels through Tokyo.

Japan is a group of more than 3,000 islands. There are four main islands: Honshu,
Hokkaido, Kyushu, and Shikoku. The highest mountain, volcanic Mount Fuji, has
a special religious meaning to the Japanese. Japan experiences many earthquakes
that damage buildings and sometimes kill people.

West Asia

There are 20 countries in West Asia. Use the key below to compare each country.

Country	Languages	Religions	Ethnic groups	Agriculture	Natural resources
Afghanistan					
Armenia					
Azerbaijan					
Bahrain					
Cyprus					
Georgia					
Iran					
Iraq					
Israel					
Jordan					
Kuwait					
Lebanon					
Oman					
Pakistan					
Qatar					
Saudi Arabia					
Syria					
Turkey					
United Arab Emirates					
Yemen					

Key

Languages
- Arabic
- Armenian
- Azerbaijani
- English
- French
- Georgian
- Greek
- Hebrew
- Kurdish
- Pakistani
- Pashtu
- Persian
- Turkik
- Turkish

Religions
- ✝ Christianity
- ☾ Islam
- ✡ Judaism

Ethnic groups
- Arab
- Armenian
- Asian
- Azeri
- Bahraini
- Georgian
- Greek
- Indian
- Jewish
- Kurdish
- Pakistani
- Pashtun
- Persian
- Tajik
- Turkish

Agriculture
- Cereal grains
- Citrus
- Coffee
- Cotton
- Dairy
- Dates
- Fruit and vegetables
- Nuts
- Olives
- Sheep, cattle, and goats
- Sugar
- Tea
- Wine and grapes

Natural resources
- Bauxite or alumina
- Coal
- Copper
- Gold
- Hydropower
- Iron ore
- Lead
- Nickel
- Oil and gas
- Phosphates
- Salt
- Timber
- Tin
- Zinc

22

Turkey in focus

Official name: Republic of Turkey

Area: 297,154 square miles
(769,630 square kilometers)

Population: 68 million

Capital: Ankara

Major cities: Istanbul, Izmir, Adana

Famous landmarks: Blue Mosque in Istanbul,
Gallipoli (World War I battleground), Mount Ararat

Famous people: Ataturk (political leader)

Traditions: Turkish music, carpet weaving, mosaics
(colorful tiles)

Traditional food: shish kebab (meat grilled on a
stick), Turkish bread, eggplant

Turkey is on the border of Asia and Europe, so
it is partly in Europe and partly in Asia. Most of
the country is in western Asia. In Asia, the land
is mainly a mountainous plateau where shepherds graze
sheep. Most people live in the western part of Turkey.
Earthquakes are common in Turkey.

A Turkish woman
making flat bread

Saudi Arabia in focus

Official name: Kingdom of Saudi Arabia

Area: 816,480 square miles
(2,114,690 square kilometers)

Population: 23 million

Capital: Riyadh

Major cities: Mecca, Abha, Al Hufuf,
Buraydah, Medina

Famous landmarks: Medina and Mecca
(Islam's holiest cities)

Famous people: King Fahd

Traditions: ardha (sword dance)

Traditional food: khobz (flat bread), falafel
(chickpea patties)

Saudi Arabia is covered by desert and takes up most of the Arabian
Peninsula. The cities of Mecca and Medina are the main centers in the
world for the Islamic religion. Every year, millions of Muslims come to
Mecca to celebrate their religion. Saudi Arabia has the world's largest
supplies of oil and gas. Money from selling oil has made many Saudi
Arabians very wealthy.

Bedouins are nomads
who travel with their
camels in the desert.

South Asia

There are 11 countries in South Asia. Use the key below to find out about and compare each country's languages, religions, ethnic groups, agriculture, and natural resources.

Country	Languages	Religions	Ethnic groups	Agriculture	Natural resources
Bangladesh					
Bhutan					
Cambodia					
India					
Laos					
Maldives					
Myanmar					
Nepal					
Sri Lanka					
Thailand					
Vietnam					

Key

Languages	Religions	Ethnic groups	Agriculture	Natural resources
Bengali	Buddhism	Bengali	Cereal grains	Bauxite or alumina
Burmese	Christianity	Bhote	Citrus	Coal
Dzongkha	Hinduism	Burman	Coffee	Copper
English	Islam	Han Chinese	Cotton	Gold
French	Traditional beliefs	Indian	Dairy	Hydropower
Hindi		Khmer	Fruit and vegetables	Iron ore
Khmer		Lao	Nuts	Lead
Lao		Minority groups	Sheep, cattle, and goats	Oil and gas
Mandarin Chinese		Nepalese	Sugar	Phosphates
Nepali		Sinhalese	Tea	Salt
Other Indian languages		Tamil		Timber
Sinhala		Thai		Tin
Tamil		Vietnamese		Zinc
Thai				
Traditional languages				
Vietnamese				

24

India in focus

Official name: Republic of India

Area: 1,147,949 square miles
(2,973,190 square kilometers)

Population: 1.1 billion

Capital: New Delhi

Major cities: Mumbai, Kolkata, Chennai, Hyderabad, Bangalore, Jaipur

Famous landmarks: Taj Mahal (building), Ganges River, Varanasi (holy city)

Famous people: Mohandas Gandhi (religious and political leader and social reformer), Sunil Gavaskar and Sachen Tendulkar (cricket players), Ravi Shankar (musician)

Traditions: Bollywood (Indian movies), sitar (musical instrument), textiles

Sorting chilies in India

Traditional food: masala (curry), tandoori, chapatis, naan and papadams (flat breads)

India has the second largest population in the world. Many Indians follow Hinduism and believe the Ganges River, which flows from the Himalayan Mountains, is sacred. Most of the vast plains are used for farming. India depends on rains from the monsoon for watering crops. Sometimes the country gets too much rain and there are severe floods.

Vietnam in focus

Official name: Socialist Republic of Vietnam

Area: 125,621 square miles
(325,360 square kilometers)

Population: 85 million

Capital: Hanoi

Major cities: Ho Chi Minh City, Da Nang, Hai Phong, Dalat, Hue

Famous landmarks: Halong Bay, Mekong River Delta

Famous people: Ho Chi Minh (political leader)

Traditions: lacquerware, painting on silk, water puppets

Traditional food: Vietnamese spring rolls, French bread rolls

Vietnamese women making traditional-style hats

Vietnam is a long country that stretches from the South China Sea to the Annam Highlands. Most Vietnamese people live in the countryside and are farmers. Rice is the main crop. The Mekong River reaches the sea in Southern Vietnam, where many people catch fish and also grow rice. Vietnam is still recovering from the long Vietnam War (1961–1975).

Southeast Asian Islands

There are six Southeast Asian Island countries. Use the key below to find out about and compare each country's languages, religions, ethnic groups, agriculture, and natural resources.

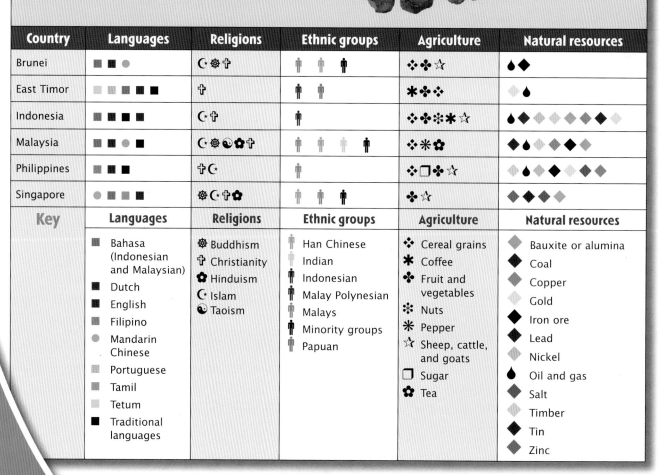

Country	Languages	Religions	Ethnic groups	Agriculture	Natural resources
Brunei	■ ■ ●	☾ ✿ ✞	👤 👤 👤	❖ ✿ ☆	💧 ◆
East Timor	■ ■ ■ ■ ■	✞	👤 👤	✳ ✿ ❖	◇ 💧
Indonesia	■ ■ ■ ■	☾ ✞	👤	❖ ✿ ✳ ✳ ☆	💧 ◆ ◇ ◆ ◆ ◆ ◆
Malaysia	■ ■ ● ■	☾ ✿ 🌙 ✿ ✞	👤 👤 👤 👤	❖ ✳ ✿	◆ 💧 ◇ ◆ ◆ ◆
Philippines	■ ■ ■	✞ ☾	👤	❖ ▢ ✿ ☆	◇ 💧 ◆ ◆ ◆ ◆
Singapore	● ■ ■ ■	✿ ☾ ✞ ✿	👤 👤 👤	✿ ☆	◆ ◆ ◆ ◆
Key	**Languages**	**Religions**	**Ethnic groups**	**Agriculture**	**Natural resources**
	■ Bahasa (Indonesian and Malaysian)	✿ Buddhism	👤 Han Chinese	❖ Cereal grains	◇ Bauxite or alumina
	■ Dutch	✞ Christianity	👤 Indian	✳ Coffee	◆ Coal
	■ English	✿ Hinduism	👤 Indonesian	✿ Fruit and vegetables	◆ Copper
	■ Filipino	☾ Islam	👤 Malay Polynesian	✳ Nuts	◇ Gold
	● Mandarin Chinese	🌙 Taoism	👤 Malays	✳ Pepper	◆ Iron ore
	■ Portuguese		👤 Minority groups	☆ Sheep, cattle, and goats	◆ Lead
	■ Tamil		👤 Papuan	▢ Sugar	◇ Nickel
	■ Tetum			✿ Tea	💧 Oil and gas
	■ Traditional languages				◆ Salt
					◇ Timber
					◆ Tin
					◆ Zinc

Indonesia in focus

Official name: Republic of Indonesia

Area: 693,700 square miles
(1,796,700 square kilometers)

Population: 212 million

Capital: Jakarta

Major cities: Surubaya, Medan, Semarang,
Denpassar, Ujungpandang

Famous landmarks: Borobudur and Prambanan
(ancient religious ruins), Bromo and Rinjani
(volcanoes)

Famous people: Suharto and Achmed Sukarno
(political leaders)

Traditions: shadow puppets, batik (printing on cloth)

Traditional food: gado gado (vegetables with peanut sauce),
nasi goreng (fried rice)

*Indonesian girls dressed
for a traditional dance*

Indonesia is the world's biggest group of islands or archipelago. They stretch for
3,100 miles (5,000 kilometers) across the ocean. The islands are mainly mountainous
with big areas of tropical rain forest. Islands such as Java, Bali, and Lombok have active
volcanoes. Indonesia has the world's third largest population. Most people live on the
main islands of Java and Sumatra.

Malaysia in focus

Official name: Federation of Malaysia

Area: 126,853 square miles
(328,550 square kilometers)

*The Petronas Towers in Kuala Lumpur is
the world's second tallest office building.*

Population: 23 million

Capital: Kuala Lumpur

Major cities: Kuching, Kota Kinabalu, Kelang, Georgetown, Johor Baharu

Famous landmarks: Mount Kinabalu, Petronas Towers

Famous people: Mahathir Mohamed (political leader)

Traditions: dance and drums, silver and brass ware, weaving

Traditional food: satay (meat on a stick with peanut sauce), nyonya
(a mix of Chinese and Malay food styles)

Malaysia is made up of three regions: Peninsular, Malaysia on the Asian
mainland, and Sabah and Sarawak on the island of Borneo. Malaysia is
mostly mountainous with areas of tropical rain forest. Most people live
in the big cities such as Kuala Lumpur. Malaysia has many different
types of people, including Indians and Chinese who started moving to
Malaysia 2,000 years ago.

Asia's future

Asia has many more people than the other continents, and the population is still growing.

Challenges

The large number of people in some Asian countries means there is not always enough food and housing for everybody. In China, the government started a **one-child policy**. This has slowed China's population growth. India is now facing the same problem and may have more people than China in 25 years' time. Countries such as Singapore and Japan have fewer people but they live in a very small area. In Japan, more than 30 million people live in Tokyo's city region and the surrounding districts.

Another big challenge for Asia is to slow the rate of rain forest clearing for farming. There are many different animals and plants living in the rain forests that are in danger of becoming extinct. Asia has developed national parks that protect animals and plants from hunting and land clearing.

The streets in Shanghai are very crowded.

28

Children in Singapore using the Internet

Goals

The goal of all Asian countries is to develop industries so that there will be more jobs for their people. China's industries are growing very fast. This means their people have more jobs and therefore, more money to spend. Many Asian countries lead the way in computer technology, which was founded in Asia by Japan and Korea. Today, South Korea has the most Internet connections in the world. Countries such as India, Malaysia, and Taiwan also make computer parts.

West Asia has the biggest supplies of oil and gas in the world. Brunei in Southeast Asia also has large supplies of oil. It is an important source of money to those countries and their people.

In some parts of Asia, wars and disputes are still going on. The goal of many Asians is to live peaceful and happy lives.

Asia in review

Asia is the biggest continent.

Area: 16.8 million square miles (43.6 million square kilometers)

Population: 3,800 million

First humans in Asia: 50,000 years ago

First civilizations: Mesopotamia and China

Other civilizations: Khmer Ottoman Empire, Moghul Empire, Japanese Imperial Dynasty

Countries: 49

Biggest country: Russia

Smallest country: Maldives

Most crowded country: Singapore

Highest point: Mount Everest at 29,030 feet (8,848 meters)

Longest river: Yangtze River in China at 3,965 miles (6,380 kilometers)

Climate zones: arctic, alpine, continental, temperate, arid, tropical

Asian regions: North Asia, West Asia, South Asia, Southeast Asian Islands

Most common languages: Mandarin, Cantonese, Hindi, Indonesian, Malaysian, Arabic, traditional languages

Web sites

For more information on Asia go to:

http://www.worldatlas.com/webimage/countrys/as.htm

http://www.atozkidsstuff.com/china.html

http://www.atozkidsstuff.com/japan.html

http://www.web-jpn.org/kidsweb/index.html

Glossary

alpine   a cold, snowy climate in high mountainous regions

arctic   extremely cold climate at or near the North Pole

Arctic Circle   an area of ice and snow located near the North Pole

arid   a dry, desert-like climate

colonized   when one country takes over another country

continental   a climate of extreme heat and cold, typical of the interior Northern Hemisphere continents

equator   an imaginary line around the middle of the Earth's surface

ethnic groups   types of people who share similar heritage

extinct   when no more of a particular species of plant or animal are left on the Earth

humid   when there is a large amount of water vapor in the air

hydropower   power made by fast-flowing water

independent   when a country governs itself

monsoon   a strong wind in and around the Indian Ocean, which brings rain

mosque   a place where Muslims worship and pray

Northern Hemisphere   the half of the Earth north of the equator

one-child policy   a law in China that only allows parents to have one child; it was introduced to slow the population growth

tectonic plates   large pieces of the Earth's crust that move slowly, causing earthquakes

temperate   a mild climate with wet weather and cool temperatures

traded   bought and sold goods

traditions   the way things have been done for many years

tropical   a hot, humid, and wet climate found near the equator

voted   the people of a country decided on something together

Index

ML

7/05